Cornerstones of Freedom

The Vietnam Women's Memorial

Deborah Kent

CHILDRENS PRESS®

CHICAGO

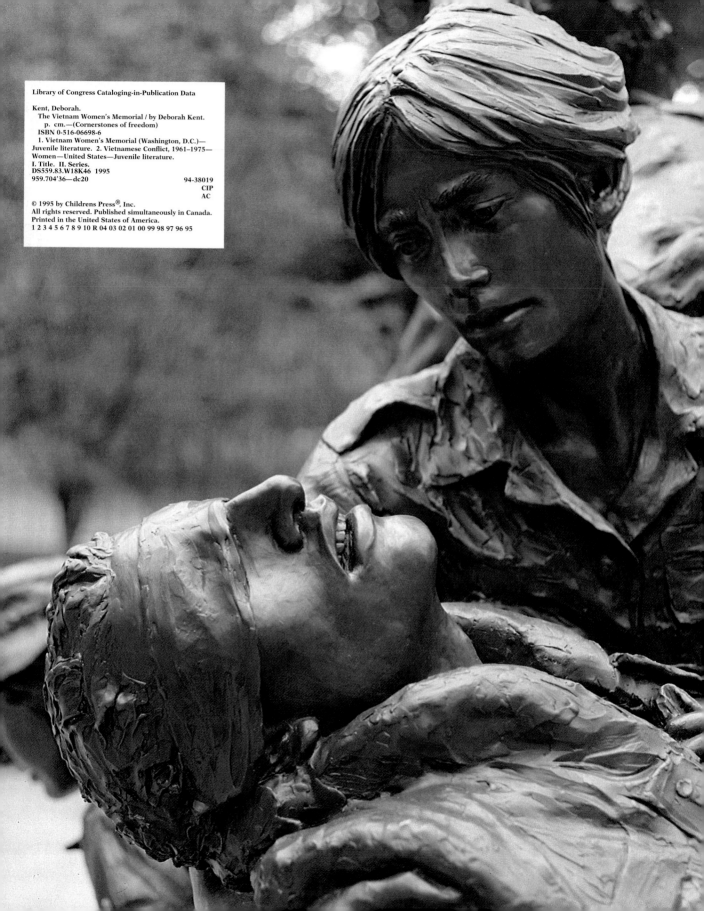

Library of Congress Cataloging-in-Publication Data

Kent, Deborah.
   The Vietnam Women's Memorial / by Deborah Kent.
      p. cm.—(Cornerstones of freedom)
   ISBN 0-516-06698-6
   1. Vietnam Women's Memorial (Washington, D.C.)—
Juvenile literature. 2. Vietnamese Conflict, 1961–1975—
Women—United States—Juvenile literature.
I. Title. II. Series.
DS559.83.W18K46 1995
959.704'36—dc20   94-38019
                                                        CIP
                                                        AC

On a gloomy day in December 1967, Mrs. Susan Orlowski of Detroit received a telegram from the Pentagon in Washington, D.C. The brief message informed her that her son had been killed in a plane crash while serving his country in Vietnam. She and her family were crushed by the tragic news.

Hedwig Orlowski is remembered at the Vietnam Women's Memorial dedication in 1993.

But Mrs. Orlowski did not have a son in the military. Instead, it was her daughter who had died. Hedwig Orlowski, an Air Force nurse, lost her life in Vietnam on November 30, 1967. The Pentagon assumed that Hedwig was a young man. At that time, military authorities scarcely acknowledged the presence of women in the Vietnam War.

Between 1965 and 1973, the United States was immersed in a brutal war in Southeast Asia. U.S. forces attempted to defeat the communist North Vietnamese and to unite Vietnam under a single government. Every evening on the TV news, Americans at home watched soldiers march out

on jungle patrol, saw planes drop bombs, and agonized over the mounting numbers of dead and wounded. But the news reports rarely mentioned the thousands of American women who served in Vietnam. People at home simply assumed that few, if any, female personnel risked their lives in Southeast Asia alongside the men.

In reality, approximately 13,000 American women served in Vietnam during the war. The exact figure is unknown, as no specific records were kept on women in the military. Most of the women who went to Vietnam were nurses with

the Army, Navy, or Air Force. Other military women worked as air traffic controllers, intelligence officers, map-makers, and clerks. No one knows how many civilian women went to Vietnam as journalists or as volunteers with the Red Cross or other organizations aiding the victims of war.

One woman who went to Vietnam at the height of the war was a twenty-two-year-old Army nurse named Diane Carlson. Diane grew up on a farm near Buffalo, Minnesota. Patriotism was very important in the Carlson family. As a teenager, Diane was deeply stirred by President John F. Kennedy's 1961 inaugural address, in which he declared, "Ask not what your country can do for you, but what you can do for your country." In the years that followed, Diane heard more and more about the fighting in Vietnam. Americans were suffering and dying in that faraway land. Diane decided to do whatever she could to help them.

After graduating from high school, Diane entered a nursing program in Minneapolis. She joined the Army as a student nurse, and underwent six weeks of basic training at Fort Sam Houston in Texas. For eight months, she worked on an orthopedic ward at Fort Lee, Virginia, caring for wounded soldiers who had been sent "stateside" for long-term treatment. All of this training, she was told, would prepare her for her final destination—Vietnam.

Diane Carlson arrived in Vietnam on a steaming day in August 1968 to begin a one-year tour of duty. Her first assignment was with a burn unit at the 36th Evacuation Hospital in the coastal town of Vung Tau. She had no previous experience with burn patients, but

Diane Carlson (right) arrived in Vietnam in 1968. She is seen here with Barbara Black, a nurse with the Australian Army Nursing Corps.

suddenly she found herself changing dressings, monitoring fluids, and watching for warning signs of infection.

"We called it OJT—on the job training," she remembered years later. "It was the young teaching the young."

At Vung Tau, Diane Carlson tended young men whose arms, legs, and even faces had been seared by white phosphorus and napalm. White phosphorus particles are burning embers that burst out of an artillery shell and bore into the skin of a victim. Napalm is a devilish concoction of jellied gasoline. Both substances produce excruciating burns.

An American-Indian nurse in Vietnam

During the Vietnam War, napalm bombs (right) killed and injured untold numbers of innocent people, including many children (left).

Most shocking of all for the young nurse was the sight of Vietnamese children on the ward whose bodies were covered with burns. Diane Carlson did not speak their language, but she tried to comfort these young patients as best she could. Still, they screamed with pain and terror at her touch. No amount of training could have prepared the Minnesota farm girl for such horrors.

Like Diane Carlson, most American women who went to Vietnam were young and eager to serve. Following orders, they arrived in full dress uniform, consisting of a two-piece suit, matching purse, and high-heeled shoes.

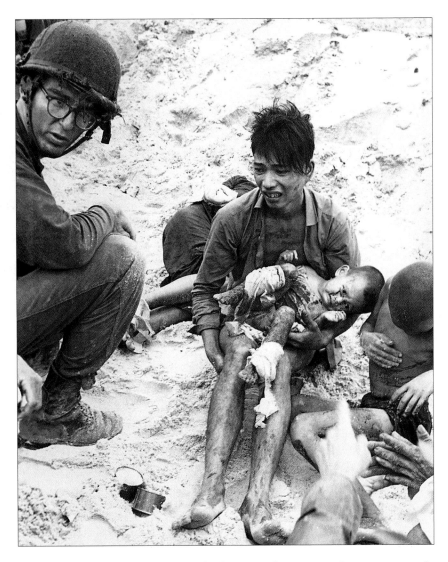

Overnight, they found themselves in the turmoil of combat. One nurse later described her arrival in Vietnam: "We were not far off the coast when the captain of the plane announced that they were shelling the airfield....The plane made a steep landing. They opened the door. We were told to follow the person in front of us into a bunker. Unfortunately, I had those high heels on. Did you ever try to run in them?"

The Vietnam conflict was a war without distinct battle fronts. There were no safe areas behind the lines. Fighting erupted anywhere—in dense jungles, in remote mountain villages, on busy city streets. Military hospitals frequently were targets for enemy shelling. During raids, nurses helped their patients crawl under beds for protection, or covered them with mattresses if they were too ill to be moved.

Far worse than the sense of personal danger was the pain of seeing so many young people with terrible injuries. The nurses cared for GIs whose legs had been blown off by exploding land mines, or whose bodies were riddled with shrapnel. "The devastating injuries just came in and came in," one nurse said later. "I remember thinking, how is it possible for people to do this to each other?"

One responsibility of the nurses in Vietnam was to boost the spirits of frightened, injured soldiers and civilians.

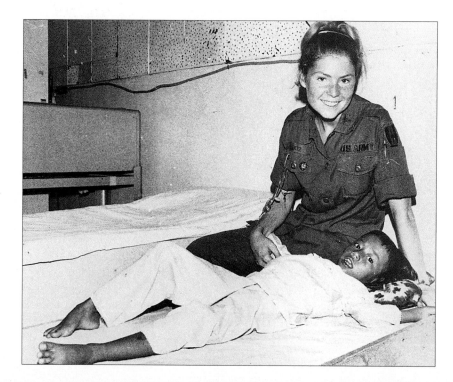

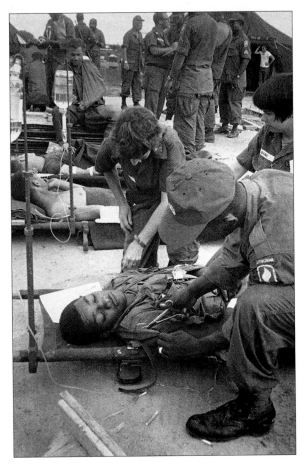

Each time the evacuation helicopters delivered a fresh cargo of sick and wounded men, the nurses began the grim process known as triage. The new patients were examined and sorted into three groups: those who could benefit most from immediate care, those who could afford to wait for help, and those who were beyond hope and must be left to die. Hopeless cases were moved out of the way, usually to a quiet corner behind a screen. Every nurse who served in Vietnam has painful memories of sitting with a dying boy, holding his hand and talking softly to him until the end.

Soldiers injured in battle were evacuated by helicopter (right) and taken to a field hospital (left). There, in triage, nurses evaluated their injuries.

By the time she was transferred to the 71st Evacuation Hospital at Pleiku, in Vietnam's central highlands, Diane Carlson had learned to keep a certain emotional distance from the young men she tended. She worked ten to fifteen hours a day, six days a week. She had no time to cry, no opportunity to mourn patients who died. Once, however, she broke her unwritten rule and promised to write to one of her patients after he returned to his fighting unit. Like Diane, Eddie was from Minnesota. While he was in the hospital, they enjoyed talking about places back home they both remembered. Diane wrote several letters to Eddie after he left the ward, but she never received an answer. One day, a package arrived at the hospital containing all of her letters, unopened. On top of the pile was a note, explaining that Eddie had been killed in action.

During her long, tumultuous year in Vietnam, Diane Carlson yearned for the peace and sanity of home. But when she returned to the States in 1969, she received no hero's welcome. The American people were disillusioned with a seemingly endless war that destroyed more and more lives every day. College campuses exploded in angry demonstrations, and the protest movement rocked the country.

Like most nurses, Carlson deplored the waste of human life she had seen in Vietnam. She

longed for the war to be over. But she was appalled when she saw protesters venting their rage on the returning veterans. The protesters seemed to be blaming the soldiers for the war. To Diane Carlson, the soldiers were not "warmongers," but victims of a conflict beyond their control. She felt the antiwar movement should focus its anger on government leaders and pressure them to bring the fighting to an end.

A few days after she returned to the family farm, Diane drove into town with her father. At the feed store, her father told the clerk, an old family friend, "Diane just got home from Vietnam." The clerk refused to look at her and would not speak.

"My dad was very embarrassed," Diane said later, "and I wanted to crawl in a hole and disappear. When we got back in the truck, I said, 'Dad, don't ever tell anybody I was in Vietnam. Just don't talk about it.'"

In the years that followed, Diane Carlson married Mike Evans, a former Army surgeon, and had four children. She tried to live as an ordinary suburban housewife, putting her year in Vietnam behind her. But haunting memories of the war kept creeping back. Sometimes she had nightmares about dying men groaning in agony. Once, helping a friend prepare food for a wedding reception, she reeled back in horror from a table covered with slabs of raw meat. The meat brought back visions of human flesh, torn with unspeakable wounds.

In 1982, Diane Carlson Evans went to Washington, D.C., to visit the newly opened Vietnam Veterans Memorial. The monument is a V-shaped wall of glossy black granite, inscribed with the names of all the American veterans who lost their lives in the Vietnam War. There are more than 58,000 names carved into the stone. Eight are the names of women who died while serving in Vietnam.

With thousands of other veterans, Diane Evans wept at the Wall as she remembered the many people she had seen die. She was especially moved when she found Eddie's name, and she paid her respects to the young man from Minnesota who never received her letters.

After her visit to the Wall, Diane's nightmares intensified. "I felt so empty," she recalled later. "I thought of all the women I had served with,

The Vietnam Veterans Memorial opened in 1982. Veterans came from across the country to visit the "Wall," which lists the names of all the Americans who were killed in the Vietnam War. Many visitors made mementos by rubbing pencil against paper and copying the names of lost friends or relatives (top).

and what we went through....I was beginning to realize the country didn't even know we were there. Vietnam was on TV, and there were the Vietnam movies, but it was all about the men.... The strangest thing, I started thinking maybe I wasn't really there. Maybe I was imagining it."

In the summer of 1983, Evans attended an exhibit of work by Minneapolis sculptor Rodger Brodin. The sculptures were realistic portrayals of soldiers in Vietnam. Evans was thrilled by Brodin's work, but disappointed that all of his subjects were men. She called him and asked if he could make a statue of a female veteran.

Brodin was intrigued by the idea. With Evans's guidance and encouragement, he spent the next five months creating the figure of an Army nurse. The nurse carried a stethoscope, scissors, and tourniquet, and in one hand she held an empty helmet.

In 1983, a statue of three male veterans, the work of sculptor Frederick Hart, was added to the grounds of the Vietnam Veterans Memorial. Evans longed to see Brodin's statue share the hallowed ground at the Wall. She felt a deep conviction that the figure of the nurse would make the memorial complete.

Together, Evans and Brodin sought the support of other veterans, especially former military nurses. Only nine people attended their first meeting, but the idea snowballed. In the spring

The statue of three male Vietnam veterans that was added at the Vietnam Veterans Memorial in 1983

of 1984, the group incorporated as the Vietnam Women's Memorial Project (VWMP) and began raising funds to make Evans's dream a reality.

During the following months, Evans and her supporters traveled throughout the country. In shopping malls and bank lobbies, at schools and churches and state fairs, they displayed a three-foot model of Brodin's statue, which veterans

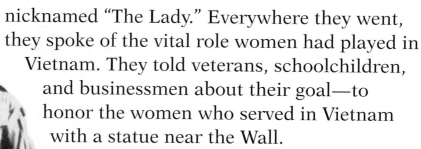

nicknamed "The Lady." Everywhere they went, they spoke of the vital role women had played in Vietnam. They told veterans, schoolchildren, and businessmen about their goal—to honor the women who served in Vietnam with a statue near the Wall.

The response was heartwarming. Contributions poured in, many accompanied by deeply moving letters. One note came from a former GI, now living in Illinois: "My most vivid memory of that day twenty-one years ago has not been of the pain from my wounds....My most vivid and fondest memory is of her, the nurse whom I will never know, but who will always hold a special place in my heart. She...cradled my hand in hers, and in a soft and caring voice all she said was, 'You'll be all right. You'll be all right.'" A child wrote: "This is all I have, but I want you to have it because if it wasn't for you my daddy wouldn't be here." Enclosed were two one-dollar bills.

Evans and her supporters quickly discovered how difficult it would be to gain approval from the government for a new memorial in Washington, D.C. In order to place Brodin's statue on the grounds of the Vietnam Veterans Memorial, they needed the approval of the Commission on Fine Arts, the National Capital Memorial Commission, and the National

Rodger Brodin's original sculpture, nicknamed "The Lady"

Capital Planning Commission. Each of these agencies had its own thorny set of requirements.

In October 1987, the VWMP faced a major hurdle—a hearing before the Commission on Fine Arts. Diane Carlson Evans and her group listened in dismay as people presented a barrage of arguments against their cause. The main objection was that if a women's memorial was erected, the Commission would likely be besieged with requests for dozens of new memorials honoring every category and group of people who served in the war. After much debate, the Commission on Fine Arts rejected the proposal by a vote of four to one.

The Vietnam Veterans Memorial wall (bottom right) is located on The Mall in Washington, D.C. It is within walking distance of many other historical monuments, including the Lincoln Memorial (top). The VWMP eventually received permission to build the Women's Memorial a short distance from the Wall.

Reeling from the blow, the VWMP delegates left the Commission's offices and retreated to a nearby restaurant. That very night, they reworked their strategy over supper. Instead of battling with each commission that controlled the monuments in the capital, they decided to push a Vietnam Women's Memorial bill through Congress. Despite their setback, they were still determined that women should be properly honored at the Wall.

Diane Carlson Evans tirelessly spearheaded letter-writing drives, made speeches, and lobbied members of Congress. Her work took her away from home for days and even weeks. Her husband was unfailingly supportive, but her absences placed a strain on family life. One day, when she returned from yet another trip to Washington, her ten-year-old son declared, "I don't care what the memorial needs right now. I have no clean jeans, and we're out of peanut butter."

Slowly, like a great, rusty machine, the legislative process moved forward. In October 1988, Congress finally passed Public Law 100-660, the Vietnam Women's Memorial Act. President Ronald Reagan signed the Act into law the following month.

Controversy still raged over the location of the memorial. The act of Congress did not clearly say that the statue should stand near the Wall. Opponents insisted it should be placed elsewhere, perhaps as far away as Arlington National Cemetery in Virginia. Another long year dragged by before President George Bush authorized a site on the grounds of the Vietnam Veterans Memorial. Bush signed the authorizing legislation on November 28, 1989.

Even then, debate surrounded the project. The Commission on Fine Arts had to grant its final approval, but the commissioners did not like The Lady. Commission director J. Carter Brown once remarked to a reporter, "The poor nurse looks like she's about to upchuck." Sadly, Diane Evans and the project staff realized they must give up any hope of using Rodger Brodin's statue. It was a bitter disappointment, but once again, they rallied their forces and moved ahead.

During the summer of 1990, the VWMP opened a nationwide design competition seeking a new statue for the memorial. The winner was a dramatic sculpture of a nurse cloaked in mist. The mist effect was to be produced by a special machine. The mist machine, however, proved to be impractical, and the judges turned to the honorable mentions. In June 1991, the VWMP board of directors announced the winning design, a statue by New Mexico sculptor Glenna Goodacre.

The groundbreaking ceremony for the Women's Memorial is held on July 29, 1993. Speaking is Diane Carlson Evans; Glenna Goodacre (right) and General Colin Powell (center) officially break ground for construction of the memorial.

Goodacre's original plan underwent a number of changes, but at last she produced a design that pleased both the commissioners and the project staff. She proposed a circular group of four connected figures conveying the passage from sorrow and fear to healing and hope. The first figure is a kneeling woman holding a helmet; she looks down with an expression of despair. Beside her, a nurse cradles a wounded soldier, his face bandaged. Next to her stands the figure of an African-American woman in military fatigues. She touches the shoulder of the nurse holding the injured man and gazes toward the sky. Some people who see the statue believe she hears an approaching helicopter. Others feel she is asking for help from God.

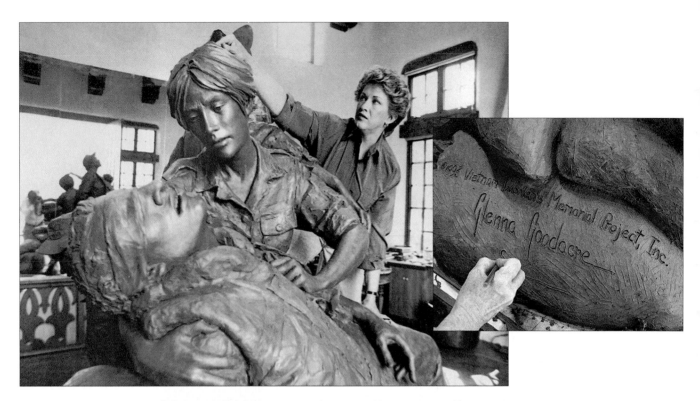

It took a year for Glenna Goodacre to sculpt the statue in clay at her New Mexico studio (top). Then it was cast in bronze in Colorado (bottom). Goodacre said of the sculpture, "The emphasis of this tribute is centered on [the women veterans'] emotions: their compassion, their anxiety, their fatigue, and above all, their dedication."

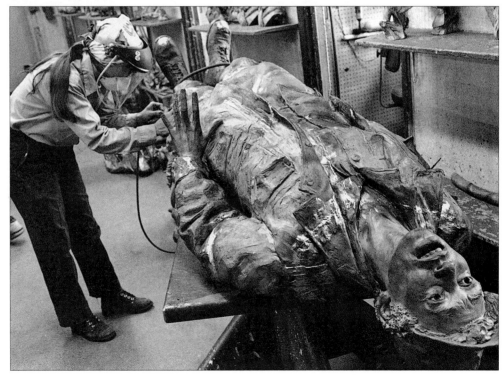

For an entire year, Glenna Goodacre worked on the bronze sculpture, which stood seven feet high when completed. In August 1993, the finished piece began its journey from her studio in Santa Fe, New Mexico. The statue was displayed in twenty-one cities along the way to its final destination, a grove of trees three hundred feet south of the Vietnam Veterans Memorial in Washington, D.C.

On Veterans Day, November 11, 1993, 25,000 people flocked to the grounds of the Vietnam Veterans Memorial to witness the dedication of the new monument. Male veterans carried placards reading "WELCOME HOME, LADIES!" Former nurses recognized long-lost friends in the crowd. It was a time of reunion, remembering, and renewal. "It's long overdue," said Marion Burkimer, a former Navy nurse. "We were supposed to be the brave ones and not have emotions. Military nurses have repressed so much!" A woman from Massachusetts commented, "They took care of our kids. Maybe somebody here took care of my boy before he died."

Vice President Al Gore delivered the keynote address to the cheering crowd: "In the tense, sometimes confusing peace that followed the Vietnam War, we never listened to these women. And we never properly thanked them. Dedicating this memorial gives us occasion to do both."

The Vietnam Women's Memorial was officially unveiled (top right; bottom) on November 11, 1993. Vice President Al Gore (top left) spoke at the dedication ceremony.

For Diane Carlson Evans, the ceremony culminated nine years of hopes and dreams and exhausting work. In her dedication address, she spoke to male veterans and to their families who had waited at home during the war. Her final words were for the women whose service was celebrated on that special day. "To my sister veterans—accept the gratitude and pride the nation now wants to bestow upon you. May it enrich your lives.... May any difficult times ahead be warmed by special memories of service to our country and knowledge that the healing power of this monument will always be here for you."

Diane Carlson Evans speaks at the dedication ceremony.

27

A male Vietnam veteran places a medal on the sculpture.

The months that followed the dedication of the Vietnam Women's Memorial gave Diane Carlson Evans time to reflect on the long campaign. She saw it as the triumph of ordinary people who had an unshakable commitment, people who refused to accept discouragement or defeat. "The story of the Vietnam Women's Memorial has something to teach us all," she states. "You *can* change the way things are. You *can* make a difference if you believe in what you are doing and get the people of America behind you. The people rule. We, the people, really do rule in the United States."

The dedication of the Women's Memorial moved women veterans to both tears and joy.

GLOSSARY

artillery – weapons that launch missiles

civilian – a person not associated with the military; many civilian women went to Vietnam as journalists or as Red Cross volunteers

communism – a political philosophy in which the state, or government, controls the economy, and all property is owned by the community, rather than by individuals; communist North Vietnam opposed democratic South Vietnam in the Vietnam War.

disillusioned – lacking enthusiasm; no longer believing in a cause

GI – term referring to soldiers in the army; abbreviation for "general infantry"

groundbreaking – a ceremony that marks the official beginning of a construction project

Napalm

evacuation – to go quickly to a safe place, to vacate

napalm – a thick, flammable gasoline substance used in bombs during the Vietnam War

orthopedic – the area of medical practice that involves healing damaged bones

shelling – bomb blasts; the noise and destruction of bomb explosions

triage – a process for sorting and treating patients before they enter a hospital

veterans – people who have served their country in war

warmonger – a person who urges his or her country into war

Veterans

white phosphorus – hot particles of exploded bombs that enter the skin

TIMELINE

North and South Vietnam split, **1954**
beginning the Vietnam conflict

1963 15,000 U.S. personnel in Vietnam

U.S. ships attacked at Gulf of Tonkin **1964**

1965 184,000 U.S. troops in Vietnam

1968

1969 President Nixon begins removing
U.S. troops from Vietnam

1973 All U.S. troops withdrawn from Vietnam

1975 South Vietnam surrenders, ending War

Diane Carlson **1976** South and North Vietnam unified
goes to Vietnam;   as communist nation
525,000 U.S.
troops in Vietnam

1982 Vietnam Veterans Memorial dedicated

1983 Statue of male soldiers added at memorial

1984 Vietnam Women's Memorial
Project (VWMP) established

1987 Commission on Fine Arts rejects proposal

Vietnam Women's Memorial Act passed **1988**

1989 Site authorized for Women's Memorial

VWMP opens competition for statue design **1990**

1991

July 29: **1993**
Groundbreaking for
Women's Memorial

November 11:
Women's Memorial dedicated

Glenna Goodacre's
design selected

INDEX *(**Boldface** page numbers indicate illustrations.)*

PHOTO CREDITS

Cover, photographed by Gregory Staley/©1993, Vietnam Women's Memorial Project, Inc., Glenna Goodacre, sculptor; 1, AP/Wide World; 2, ©Mae Scanlan; 3, ©Rick Reinhard/Impact Visuals; 4, 5 (center), AP/Wide World; 5 (right), UPI/Bettmann; 6, 7 (bottom), AP/Wide World; 7 (top), Courtesy Diane Carlson Evans; 8 (both photos), UPI/Bettmann; 9, 10, AP/Wide World; 11 (both photos), 13, 15 (center), UPI/Bettmann; 15 (top), ©Rick Reinhard/Impact Visuals; 15 (bottom), 17, 18, 19, 20, AP/Wide World; 22, UPI/Bettmann; 23, AP/Wide World; 24 (top left), ©Steve Northrup; 24 (top right and bottom), ©Daniel Anthony; 26 (top), AP/Wide World; 26 (left), ©Rick Reinhard/Impact Visuals; 26 (bottom), Reuters/Bettmann; 27, ©Rick Reinhard/Impact Visuals; 28, AP/Wide World; 29, ©Andrew Lichtenstein/ Impact Visuals; 30 (top), UPI/Bettmann; 30 (bottom), ©Andrew Lichtenstein/Impact Visuals; 31 (left), Courtesy Diane Carlson Evans; 31 (top right), AP/Wide World; 31 (bottom right), ©Steve Northrup

ADDITIONAL PICTURE IDENTIFICATIONS

Cover: *The Vietnam Women's Memorial*
Page 1: *At the dedication ceremony for the Vietnam Women's Memorial, two Vietnam veterans place flowers on the sculpture.*
Page 2: *Detail of the Vietnam Women's Memorial sculpture*

STAFF

Project Editor: Mark Friedman
Design & Electronic Composition: TJS Design
Photo Editor: Jan Izzo
Cornerstones of Freedom Logo: David Cunningham

ABOUT THE AUTHOR

Deborah Kent grew up in Little Falls, New Jersey, and received her B.A. from Oberlin College. She earned a master's degree in social work at Smith College, and worked for four years at the University Settlement House on New York's Lower East Side.

  Ms. Kent left social work to begin a career in writing. She published her first novel, *Belonging*, while living in San Miguel de Allende, Mexico. She has written a dozen novels for young adults, as well as numerous nonfiction titles for children. She lives in Chicago with her husband and their daughter, Janna.